NASCAR ★
Racing

WITHDRAWN

Paul Challen

PowerKiDS
press.

New York

Published in 2015 by **The Rosen Publishing Group, Inc.**
29 East 21st Street, New York, NY 10010

Library of Congress Cataloging-in-Publication-Data

Challen, Paul C. (Paul Clarence), 1967-
 NASCAR racing / Paul Challen.
    pages cm. — (Checkered Flag)
 Includes index.
 ISBN 978-1-4994-0174-5 (pbk.)
 ISBN 978-1-4994-0132-5 (6 pack)
 ISBN 978-1-4994-0164-6 (library binding)
 1. Stock car racing—United States—Juvenile literature.
 2. NASCAR (Association)—History—Juvenile literature. I. Title.
 GV1029.9.S74C425 2015
 796.72—dc23

                        2014033942

Developed and produced for Rosen by BlueAppleWorks Inc.
Art Director: T. J. Choleva
Managing Editor for BlueAppleWorks: Melissa McClellan
Designer: Joshua Avramson
Photo Research: Jane Reid
Editor: Joanne Randolph

Photo Credits: cover, title page, p. 25 left Beelde Photography/Shutterstock; TOC Christa Leigh Thomas/
Dreamstime; p. 4–5 bottom ciapix/Shutterstock; p. 5 right Denton Rumsey/Shutterstock; p. 6 top, p. 6–7 bottom
Public Domain/Library of Congress; p. 7 top David T. Foster, III/Keystone Press; p. 8 top, 11 left, 12–13 bottom, 13,
15, 18 top right, 20 top, 24 left Action Sports Photography/Shutterstock; p. 9 right Doug James/Dreamstime;
p. 10 left Cathy McKinty/Acclaim Imagery; p. 11 right Warren Rosenberg/Dreamstime; p. 12 top, p. 10–11 bottom
Matthew Jacques /Shutterstock; p. 12 middle, 26 left, 27 right Daniel Raustadt/Dreamstime; p. 14–15 bottom ©
Joe Burbank/Keystone Press; p. 14 top Royalbroil/Creative Commons; p. 15 left JGkatz|Jeffrey G. Katz/Creative
Commons; p. 16 top and bottom, p. 8–9 bottom, 16–17 middle, 19 right, 26 right, 27 left, 28 top Walter Arce/
Dreamstime; p. 17 right spirit of america/Shutterstock; p. 18–19 bottom, p. 18 left Lawrence Weslowski Jr/
Dreamstime; p. 20 left Christopher Halloran/Shutterstock; p. 22–23 bottom Christa Leigh Thomas/Dreamstime;
p. 23 right Photo Works/Shutterstock; p. 24–25 bottom Macleoddesigns/Dreamstime; p. 25 right Darryl Moran/
Creative Commons; p. 28–29 bottom Skip Barber Racing School/www.skipbarber.com; p. 28 left Gunter Nezhoda/
Dreamstime; p. 29 top Barry Blackburn/Shutterstock

Manufactured in the United States of America
CPSIA Compliance Information: Batch #CW15PK: For Further Information contact: Rosen Publishing, New York, New York at 1-800-237-9932

Table of Contents

What Is NASCAR?

NASCAR is a series of car races held all over the United States, Canada, Mexico, and Europe. It is very popular, with fans in more than 150 countries around the world watching the races on television in 20 languages.

The cars that race in NASCAR are known as **stock cars**. These are cars built by major manufacturing companies for regular use, rather than cars made especially for racing. Modifications to the cars' engines and bodies get them ready to race at speeds of up to 200 miles per hour (320 km/h).

Thousands of fans attend NASCAR races every year.

NASCAR Races

Races are run at different lengths, with the most famous ones ranging from 200 to 600 miles (320 to 966 km) long. They are usually held on oval **tracks** anywhere from about a quarter-mile (.4 km) in length to close to three miles (4.8 km). Different types of races include short track, speedway, superspeedway, and road courses.

WHAT DOES "NASCAR" MEAN?

NASCAR stands for the National Association for Stock Car Auto Racing. Its home base is in Daytona Beach, Florida, and it has offices in eight cities across North America. From its humble beginnings, NASCAR has grown into a hugely popular organization. Only the National Football League has more TV viewers in the United States. And what's more, NASCAR estimates that it holds 17 of the 20 most popular one-day sports events in the world!

The NASCAR Hall of Fame is in Charlotte, North Carolina.

The History of NASCAR

People started racing regular cars informally in the early part of the 20th century. They soon realized they could make changes to the cars' engines and other parts to make them go faster. They could make the races safer and more interesting, too, if they adopted competitive rules and planned organized races.

Horse racing tracks were often used as racetracks for early car races.

There were few rules when car racing first appeared. An empty road and a group of daredevils was all it took.

Family affair

In 1947, a group of drivers including a man named Bill France formed NASCAR as a series of stock car races. They were called stock cars because they were not specially made for racing. They used the same frame as a family car. "Big Bill" France and his early partners believed by developing this series they would help car racing become more popular. They thought that racing cars people could own themselves would bring in more fans. By 1949, France's wish came true. Today, France's grandson has taken over NASCAR.

Big Bill's grandson Brian France is the Chairman and CEO of NASCAR.

NASCAR Series

NASCAR races are divided into groups of races known as series. These series are named after the companies that sponsor them by providing prize money and covering other costs.

The NASCAR Sprint Cup Series teams take to the track at the Indianapolis Motor Speedway.

The Sprint Cup Series is considered the highest level of stock car racing. For each race, drivers earn points depending on how high they finish and how many laps they lead. After 26 races, the top 16 drivers in wins and points qualify for the Chase for the Sprint Cup. The Chase consists of 10 races; 12 drivers are eliminated during the first nine Chase races. In the last race, the highest finisher of the final four drivers wins the series. Although only Chase drivers can win the Sprint Cup, every Chase race features all the drivers in the series.

The Nationwide Series is the series for up-and-coming drivers in NASCAR. These "future stars" race cars that are slightly smaller and less powerful than those in the Sprint Cup.

Nationwide Series races are often held on a day before the Sprint Cup race to encourage fans to attend both events.

Truck series

The Camping World Truck Series is different from most NASCAR races in that modified pickup trucks compete instead of cars. The series began in 1995 after pickup truck races had been run as demonstrations at NASCAR events.

GOING INTERNATIONAL

NASCAR has become very popular in countries other than the U.S. To keep fans in other countries excited about the sport, NASCAR organizes series like the Canadian Tire Series in Canada, the Mexico Toyota series in Mexico, and the Whelen Euro Series in Europe.

The Camping World Truck series is the only series in all of NASCAR to race modified production pickup trucks.

The Car

A stock car has three main parts: the body, the chassis (frame), and the engine. The entire vehicle weighs 3,400 pounds (1,542 kg). NASCAR has many rules about how racing teams can modify cars, and they can be quite complicated. Basically, a modified stock car will typically have changes made to its chassis, suspension, and engine that will all combine to make each car in a race equal in its performance ability and top speed. Makes of cars used in NASCAR races include Ford, Chevrolet, Dodge, and Toyota.

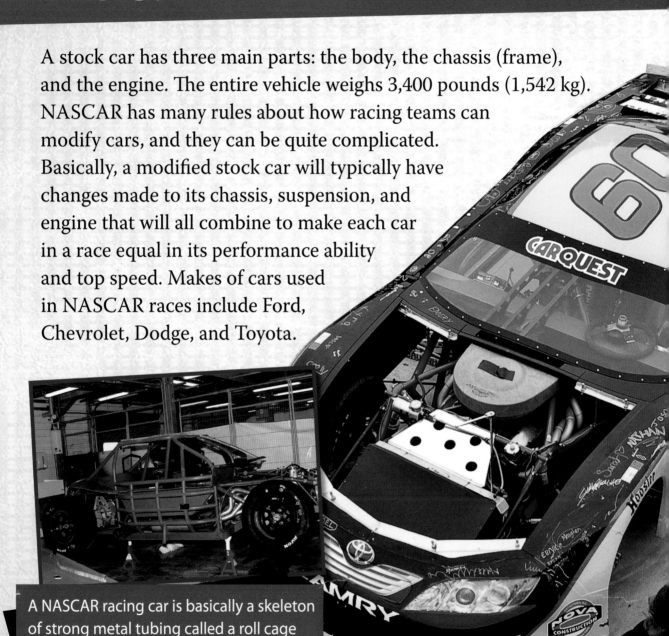

A NASCAR racing car is basically a skeleton of strong metal tubing called a roll cage covered with metal sheeting.

Engines and tires

When they are modified, engines used in NASCAR Sprint Cup races can generate up to 850 horsepower (hp). That is very powerful, especially when you consider that the average family car or van generates around 200 hp!

ENTRY POINT
Drivers enter a stock car through the front window. There are actually no doors on a stock car – the sides are made of a single sheet of metal, reinforced for safety.

Goodyear Tire & Rubber Company is the sole supplier to all three major racing series.

NASCAR driver Kyle Busch entering his racing car.

Stock car tires do not have any treads. They are smooth so the car can go as fast as possible. They are filled with nitrogen instead of air. In a typical race weekend, a NASCAR race team can use between nine and fourteen sets of tires depending on the length and type of the race.

The Driver

With all the cars being more or less equal, the ability of the drivers and their teams is the most important factor in a race. NASCAR racing demands that these drivers be in great shape. They must also be able to concentrate for several hours in very hot track temperatures of up to 120 °F (49 °C).

A NASCAR driver discusses the race plan with one of his team members.

Winning a race is not a matter of just driving as fast as you can for an entire race. Drivers need an overall plan, or **strategy**, for the race, which they set before the start. They also use **tactics**, such as drafting or slipstreaming, which involves driving close behind another car to save energy by letting the car in front push into the air and wind.

The whole team celebrates when a NASCAR driver wins a race.

Suiting up

Drivers also need to be mentally alert at all times as many of their decisions need to be made very quickly. One wrong move can easily lead to an accident! To protect themselves, drivers wear high-impact helmets, the HANS device (Head and Neck Support device), and **fire-retardant** full-body suits and boots. No driver wants to be involved in a crash, but this equipment offers maximum protection if one happens.

Special seats in NASCAR race cars wrap around the driver's rib cage. This provides extra support during a crash.

The Track

There are four basic types of NASCAR tracks:

- superspeedways
- short tracks
- standard ovals
- road courses

Short track racing is often associated with fairgrounds and similar fun occasions.

A superspeedway is a long track, at least 2 miles (3.2 km) in length. Because they are so long, cars can reach very high speeds on them. There are seven superspeedway tracks in the United States.

A short track is one that is less than 1 mile (1.6 km) long. Many drivers looking to climb the ranks of NASCAR get their start on short tracks. Most NASCAR races on short tracks are 400 to 500 laps long.

Pickup trucks pull massive jet dryers to dry the **Daytona International Speedway** before a race.

MY RACETRAV

The standard oval track is often one mile (1.6 km) long, though its length can vary.

A road course provides a different challenge, since they have many turns, and both right and left turns. The NASCAR Sprint Cup Series races at two road courses every year: Watkins Glen International in New York and Sonoma Raceway in California.

Oval tracks are dedicated motorsport circuits, used mainly in North America.

Sonoma Raceway in California is a road course that hosts one of the NASCAR Sprint Cup Series races each year.

⚠ FAST FACT

It is very dangerous for stock cars to race on wet tracks. So NASCAR uses technology called the Air Titan to dry the tracks off. The Air Titan blows hot, compressed air onto the track to dry it. A pickup truck tows the Titan around the track.

Famous Tracks

NASCAR race sites are huge. The biggest one is the Indianapolis Motor Speedway. It has room for almost 250,000 people, making it the biggest single sports venue in North America.

Talladega Superspeedway

One of the legendary NASCAR tracks is the Daytona International Speedway in Florida. The Daytona 500, the first race each year on the NASCAR circuit, was first held there in 1959.

Located in Alabama, the Talladega Superspeedway is also one of the most famous NASCAR venues. It was built on a former US Air Force base and is well-known among fans for the steep banks of its turns.

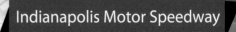
Indianapolis Motor Speedway

Charlotte Motor Speedway

Daytona International Speedway

The Charlotte Motor Speedway, located in North Carolina, is famous for hosting such races as the Coca-Cola 600, the Bank of America 500, and the Sprint All-Star race. There is also a drag strip at the race course.

The Watkins Glen International course, in Watkins Glen, New York, is well-known as a course for all kinds of racing, including NASCAR. Originally races were held on local roads, but a permanent course for auto racing was built there in 1956.

Race Day

Sunday is usually the "big day" for NASCAR fans. There is much more to experience than just the race! There is often a pre-race show that can include a concert, a military tribute, and introductions to the drivers taking part.

There's always a chance you can get an autograph from your favorite driver at a race day.

To add to the day's fun, around the track there are cars on display and stands where fans can buy refreshments and souvenirs.

Before drivers can race in the Sunday finals, they must go through a series of qualifying rounds. The driver who records the fastest qualifying time starts in the "pole position." In the race, a pace car is often used during times when it is unsafe for the drivers to race, such as poor weather conditions or when there is debris on the track. The pace (or "safety") car drives in front of the car leading the race, and no drivers are allowed to pass it until the caution is lifted.

TEAM SPIRIT

Stock car racing is costly. Teams count on sponsors to help cover costs and to provide prize money for winning races. Each driver in a NASCAR race is part of a team, sponsored by a company or companies who pay to have their logo put on the cars and on the clothing of the driver and crew. It can cost a lot of money to sponsor some of NASCAR's favorite drivers, such as Dale Earnhardt Jr. In 2013, the Army National Guard spent $30 million to have their logo on Earnhardt's car.

Earnhardt was voted NASCAR's most popular driver by fans for the 11th straight year in 2013.

Racing Rules

NASCAR races follow a basic set of rules. For example, each race covers a set amount of laps, and a certain number of cars race in each final. Rules also cover how many points a driver and team gain in each race, and how drivers must race one another safely.

The checkered flag is one any driver would like to see. It means the winner has crossed the finish line!

Race organizers use a system of **flags** to show the drivers and their teams what is happening on the track. For example, a green flag means the race is on, and drivers can race at full speeds. A red flag means the race must stop.

A pace car limits the speed of competing cars on a racetrack.

When the yellow caution flag comes out, NASCAR drivers are "frozen" in position and must follow the pace car in that position until the caution is removed. The car that is leading must slow down to let the pace car take up the lead position at this point, or face a penalty.

NASCAR Racing Flags

The flagman is a NASCAR official who waves different colored flags at the drivers to give them race information. He sits in a special seat above the start/finish line so all the drivers can see him. Here is what the flags he waves mean:

Green Flag
The start of a race or all-clear track conditions.

Red Flag
The race has been stopped. Drivers reduce their speed and proceed with caution to a designated stopping area.

Black Flag
Displayed to one driver, the driver has 5 laps to respond to a concern from NASCAR.

Black Flag with Diagonal White Stripe
Displayed to a driver who has not pitted his car after being shown the black flag. This flag indicates the car is disqualified until they pit.

Yellow Flag
There is a potentially hazardous situation; drivers slow down and keep their position.

Light Blue Flag with Diagonal Yellow Stripe
The driver is about to be overtaken by faster drivers and must yield to them.

White Flag
The final lap of a race for the race leader.

Checkered Flag
The end of a race or practice session. Drivers move around the track or course to the designated exit.

The Pit Stop Hustle

The most powerful tool a NASCAR driver has is his car—but his car wouldn't survive even one race without the care it gets in the **pit** from the crew. Drivers service their cars during pit stops. Pit areas are located off the racetrack, along the pit road. Racing at high speeds is very tough on cars. Stock cars need to stop several times during a race for gas and fresh tires. The pit crew does all of this work.

A pit crew is made up of twelve members. Seven are allowed over the concrete wall and onto the pit road. The other five must stay behind the wall. These five may hand tools back and forth to the other members. Each pit crew member has one job. Jobs include refueling, changing tires, and cleaning windows.

The pit crew must work fast. Even the fastest drivers can lose a race because of a long pit stop.

Every Second Counts

Pit crew members need to be good at what they do and work fast. During a race, every second counts. If the car spends too long in the pits, valuable racing time is lost. They need to be able to change four tires, add a full tank of fuel, and clean the windows in about twelve seconds.

KEEPING IT CLEAN

The windshields on NASCAR race cars are made of the material used on fighter-plane canopies. This material is very strong. It does not shatter when an object hits it. Unlike the windshield of a regular car, NASCAR windshields are cleaned simply by having a pit crew member tear away a clear plastic sheet when it gets dirty. The plastic sheets have tabs on them so it is easy to peel one off to reveal another underneath.

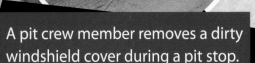

A pit crew member removes a dirty windshield cover during a pit stop.

Crash Course

Because the cars are moving so fast and close together in a NASCAR race, crashes happen often. It is common to see collisions involving several cars at once. NASCAR has made many changes to cars and racetracks to make drivers safer. For example, cars are equipped with a special frame around the driver called a roll cage. It is made from heavy-duty materials to prevent injury. The car's seat wraps around the driver's rib cage to protect him or her as well.

The HANS (Head and Neck Support) system is a special device that protects a driver's head and neck. It sits on top of the shoulders, behind the helmet. Strong seatbelts are also used in NASCAR cars to protect drivers.

NASCAR cars are equipped with a variety of safety devices that protect the driver.

DALE EARNHARDT

On February 18, 2001, Dale Earnhardt died in a crash at the Daytona 500. Earnhardt was one of the legendary NASCAR drivers. He won a total of 76 races over the course of his career and was considered one of the best NASCAR drivers of all time. Since Earnhardt's death, there have been many safety changes made. No driver in a NASCAR cup series has died in a race since then.

Dale Earnhardt was inducted into the NASCAR Hall of Fame on May 23, 2010.

The HANS device is a safety item required in many car racing sports.

NASCAR Stars

It takes many hours of practice and hard work to become a top driver. Many famous drivers have raced for several years before their first win, and all of them have expert pit crews backing them up.

JEFF GORDON

Named to NASCAR's 50 Greatest Drivers, Jeff Gordon began racing very small cars when he was only four years old. He is also active in raising money for sick children.

JIMMIE JOHNSON

Jimmie Johnson drives the No. 48 Lowe's/Kobalt Tools Chevrolet SS.

A true legend of NASCAR, Jimmie Johnson won NASCAR Cup titles from 2006 to 2010, and again in 2013. In 2009, after his fourth consecutive title, he was named US Athlete of the Year by the Associated Press, the first NASCAR driver to win that honor.

Jeff Gordon drives the No. 24 Chevrolet SS for Hendrick Motorsports.

TONY STEWART

Winner of the NASCAR Sprint Cup Championship in 2002, 2005, and 2011, Tony Stewart has also competed successfully in IndyCar racing. Stewart has also become popular for his many appearances on TV shows and commercials, and as the host of his own radio program.

Stewart owns and drives the No. 14 Bass Pro Shops/Mobil 1 Chevrolet SS.

WOMEN OF NASCAR

Many forms of racing have prohibited women drivers. But NASCAR has allowed women to race since the beginning, although no woman has ever won an official race.

Today, Danica Patrick has become a top driver on the circuit and has also been very successful in IndyCar racing, winning the 2008 Indy Japan 300 race. She won the award for NASCAR Nationwide Series' most popular driver in 2012.

In the 2013 season, Danica Patrick drove the No. 10 GoDaddy.com Chevrolet SS.

You and NASCAR

You can be a part of NASCAR racing, although you may be too young to actually drive in races. It is easy to watch races on TV and there may be a racetrack in your area that you can visit. Just remember to bring your earplugs!

Watching your favorite driver in action is always a great thrill.

Another great way to follow NASCAR is to follow your favorite driver. You can keep track of how he or she is doing in races and in the standings of **cup competitions**.

If you are interested in trying racing yourself, you can begin with go-karts. Many NASCAR drivers started this way, and it's great practice for bigger, faster cars.

Many famous race drivers started out with kart racing at a young age.

Driver's Education

Remember that getting a good education in school is also important for a NASCAR driver. Learning to drive a high-tech car, understanding complicated race instructions, working as part of a team, and being able to talk to the media are skills you begin to learn in school.

It's also important that drivers be in top physical shape to keep up with the demands of races, so keep fitness in mind as well!

You and your parents can have fun together at fairs featuring mini NASCAR cars.

Another way to learn about racing is to attend a racing school. It will give you the opportunity to drive and understand car racing.

Drive. Race. Win.

Glossary

cup competition A series of races in which points are awarded for wins and laps led; the driver in first place at the end of the season wins the cup, or trophy.

Daytona International Speedway NASCAR's best-known track, located in Florida.

fire-retardant Having to do with being able to slow or stop the spread of flames in a fire.

flag A device used in NASCAR by officials to signal instructions to drivers

NASCAR The National Association for Stock Car Auto Racing, the leading organization for stock car racing in the world.

pit The part of the track where cars stop for repair, refueling and tire changes.

roll cage A safety feature on stock cars that protects the driver's side of the car.

stock car A car that has been modified from its original factory condition for racing.

strategy A plan to reach a certain goal.

tactics Specific ways or methods used to reach goals.

track The racecourse for stock cars and other forms of auto racing.

For More Information

Further Reading

Buckley Jr., James. *NASCAR.* DK Children, 2005.

Mahaney, Ian F. *The Math of NASCAR.* Powerkids Press, 2011.

Roberts, Angela. *NASCAR's Greatest Drivers.* Random House Books for Young Readers, 2009.

Websites

Due to the changing nature of Internet links, PowerKids Press has developed an online list of websites related to the subject of this book. This site is updated regularly. Please use this link to access the list: **www.powerkidslinks.com/tcf/NASCAR**

Index